OLD
SAVAGE
- - - - - - - - -
YOUNG
CITY

Nathaniel Tarn

Random House
New York

ACKNOWLEDGMENTS

Some of these poems have appeared, or will shortly appear, in
the following reviews and anthologies: *Agenda; Ambit; Chelsea*
(U.S.A.) ; *The Cheltenham Festival of Literature Handbook,
1963; Developmental Medicine and Child Neurology; Endor;
The Listener; New British Writing* (U.S.A.) ; *The Observer;
Outposts; The Pattern of Poetry; Poetry & Audience;
The Poetry Review; A Review of English Literature; Stand;
The Transatlantic Review* (U.S.A.) ; *Tribune; X;* and some have
been broadcast in "The Poet's Voice" and other features on
the B.B.C. Third Programme. To the Editors of all these my
acknowledgments are due.

Contents

to my East

One

GRIEF IS SO MUCH A NOW

Grief is so much a now –
the hand has not moved, and will not move –
yet the hand moves as the spine scores the earth
it weighs on, as the skull fits rock sockets, the toes
recollect that this is grass, this leaf, this twig,
as the eye roams its zenith for the eagle who will cross it
preserving his kingdom against all intrusions.

Grief is so much a now – things cry, believe me,
I have heard them. I have heard their complaint
as the hand and the eye assess them in turn.
If it would seem to you that none is linked to another,
that there is no relation between any of them,
as you go about your daily business: remember
that, at certain times, they cry all together as a choir.

The things of grief, her detailed catalogues,
are a present you will never lose; they will ensure
that you can never die. Each item floats one fare!
Grief is so much a now – that you swim with or against
the tide, no matter – as you open your mouth to cry too,
the waters that move backwards and forwards in you,
each wave of these waters you are proposes her name.

OUT OF SLEEP, BEYONDED

Bread, granted directly from the hand,
requites no prayer.
                              Whose hand?
Out of dreams, via waking, on tongue-
tip; out of sleep, beyonded,
like drowned swimmers past revival
yet the heaviest dead of all or
certain fish fishermen discuss
but never see; from the anonymous drift –
the hoverers in sargasso layers
laid with the dust and carriage
of the deep – the very hand rises
or thought in hand I hardly tell:
                              And must be
disencumbered – verb from root extracted,
then marshalled, mouthed continuously, re-
peated over and over as the day
jerks into place (the primal movements:
feeding and communion) until it can
be written down and stared at whole.
                              For, without this,
it will back out of grasp like a crab,
like all that's alien, sea-begotten,
that cannot breathe outside the sea
and holding converse with the drowned.

TO THE STILLNESS OF

It has been dawning on me, day by day,
that this is the way it is going to be from now on,
inescapably: a matter of digging down to
the hidden roots of,
the stillness, the breathless quiet of –

the pages of my brain are leaden and getting heavier,
their text is as cruel as braille;
the books in my head are as blind as the hooded faces of,
as I run my fingers tentatively over them –

this is what one saw in his flaming bush, another
in his hills and valleys, a third in his kiln-baked bones,
what some of us peer to see in tea leaves, bread and wine,
birds' guts, the hiccuping stars, the to and fro
of waves, frogs in a rippling pond, the plucked daisy;

some try to hear in music beating
or the heart: a downward lunge of the hand after the spirit
and a bringing back of words and their manifold readings.
Pay now, have later.

It is a reaching down into the underlying stillness of,
unbought, unpaid for, unreceipted,
a placing of the hand by a doctor under the chest muscles
and warming the sublime pulse of the mystery of – until
beating, announcing, telling the truth beads one after
another,
what was not hitherto known, purchased, secure, is: Have now.

BRING A CHILD FLOWERS

Bring a child flowers: pluck them from the air,
cut them in gardens, buy them at corner stalls,
smart shops – all one. Her smile is of one price.

If you can explain to me how it comes about
that one can adore so and wish to cripple so
in one same moment one's own life's fingers,
one's mornings' reapers, the weavers of one's nights –
I think some other poet said: I love, and hate
and I am miserable without understanding of this human state –
tell me with this one smile how it can be.

When I can still my nerve to her pace,
she is such gold, such reward,
not shrill at all.

The border of heaven and hell this very moment
(though I'm full of good will to bursting) reels on a nerve
which falls like a rod straight through my guts.
We do not go from health into disease
and back again to health. We crawl like animals,
nursing the worms will eat them later on,
from pain to pain. And pain's nerve runs here:

a frontier on which love and rage confuse their documents,
a no man's land in which the pass of love
meanders like my child from smiles to tears.

Do tell my children please, in black on white,
that once, when I was young and close to them,
I loved them as a god must love his fantasies
and laid my hands upon them while they slept,

willing my love to fashion in my hands
such rainbow sprays of covenanted time
as reached one season when, flower-like, they wilted

into the men and women who do not know me.

THE FINERIES

Let the men leap about like idiots as usual,
posture, joke and holler, they'll soon tire.
Let the women get to and try on the fineries.

If the forest had come alive, if the trees had faces
high up in their leaves, if the drowned had eyes
playing with light and spume on the surface waters;
if the Amazon had come in person to winter's London
and brought her robes to town and her feathered jewels,

our host could have matched her with his box of fineries.
One with waist-long hair played Rima in the jungle,
one thought 'I'm less ugly than I've always believed',
a third danced silently with her hands to her ears –
I said 'for my cash, it's Rima any day' ...

Nobody saw the apes had come down from the trees.

HEAD WITH HELMET

A white globe at rest in the spin of the world
it will leave. At rest, cushioned and nursed,
still, still as a white rind, a new-laid egg.
Still and ready to burst. An egg, too large by inches
for the chick it holds: earth's buoyancy in space.
The vizor: Cyclops' single, gapes upwards,
purblind in yawning to the light it drinks
yet cannot relish. The vizor: stiff, immoveable
and locked on target. But behind it, frail, and leaning
down, right out of course, the lovely smile of man,
chin barely grazing shoulder, splinters goodbye
for parent, infant, lover, colleague, you.
Goodbye. To break no differently, no younger
certainly, than broke let's say six hundred years ago
when, coffined in his steel, a man for Marion
or honour smiled down like this at his last grass.

RANGER SPACECRAFT

Where the report says it stops and 'parks'
after the first whoosh which scalds Canaveral
and hoists the whole of Florida, America even, above
that ink sea seared with orange the big jets bask on
into a fire we can no more imagine – there,
where it shifts on its axis, shoots out antennae,
shivers the cold off its flanks, appears to think,
appears to meditate on the earth's commandments,
where it still seems to belong to us, has not left us
entirely, is where I cannot help thinking of it
as of a creature outbound in heart-breaking loneliness.
When geese set out on their rapt orbits round the sky
or schools of whales furrow the aching sea,
they seem alone to us, yet have their company:
none is so lonely as that human star. That it is of man,
shine of his brain, of his fine hands finished,
that it bears such questions with it, such probes,
that it makes us turn from our hearts to what we know
and causes us to learn that we do not know, is compassion.
Take the lobster from its cave as it measures with claws
the enveloping squid and lacks salvation's span
and knows its carapace will not save it, but knows how?
Take the slush of a houseless crab on the shark's tooth,
the rabbit mumbling at the rattler's open jaw,
the fledgeling skewered on the eagle's talon –
take all that faces dying and may still ask questions.
How do they know? How do their limbs contract?
How do they gaze out, their thoughts move at the end?

MASTER SPY

They stay at home most days washing white gloves,
sheening top hats, freshening up ribbons,
polishing boots, belts, wallets.
Their uniforms are always to hand.
You can spot them, on outings, a mile off.

I wear rags like the heart.

They have people in to clean their drains, ram free
potsherds, builders' cement, the coal of snow.
Their drains are rubbed almost transparent.
You can see codes, messages, declarations,
whispers, running through them as in a stream.
From the next house, my ear sucking the wall,
I hear and know that tongue of theirs forever –
I spoke it once, took my ease in it, my comfort,
when the whole world could speak it with lions and lambs.

It stutters vexed now like blood to the heart.

Listen. Swallow to free your ears. Try to hear me.
We shall meet again very soon and converse once more.
I shall be able to translate the entire language for you.
You will grasp the tenor of whole phrases, even paragraphs.
I shall make clear to you the meaning of this war.

Your heart will start ticking over very gently again.

NOMAD

I shall square the circle: uproot each sentiment,
hack out my heart from its beating place,
rather than be a son to righteousness.
And that is all the tending I will do, the tilling and ploughing.
He was righteous. This is granted. Please accept it.
I mean his grid maps were correct; he had it all parcelled out:
he knew just where each channel should flow and at what hour,
also the rotation of crops for the best aggregate yield.
Cases were brought to him for trial. He was his own lawyer.
He would even know that so and so's son should raise such a crop,
another be raised ... taught this or that trade. He even cared
something for the earth.

But I want the lovely earth to flower and my cattle to graze
and laze along in a frieze along the sky just as they are.

The heart's quintessence, let me tell you, is not of righteousness:
love is not written down with paper and ink –
not drained like that.
Your harvests in the end leaned all one way.
Everything round him wilted as in too hot a sun.

I too am woven of pity and mercy but will not yield up this sword.

I am to forget his appalling courage and forgo all his results:
if not I wilt, if not I die too, my pastures, my cattle too.

LAST OF THE CHIEFS

I speak from ignorance.
Who once learned much, but speaks from ignorance now.
Who trembled once with the load of such knowledge,
trembled and cried and gritted his teeth and gripped
with his fists the ends of the arms of his throne.

Who once distilled this island in his green intestines
like the whale distils her dung gone dry called ambergris –
a perfume for faraway races

who wrecked us.

Only here and there, like lightning before the rain's whips,
like a trench along the deep, a thought such as I had:

in the belly of the whale there is room for such an island.

I laugh. I come now. I clear space. My name, my very being
is that: I clear space. I pass over them with my thongs, laughing,
that have died fighting the island-bellied whale, not prevailed,
turned at last their steels against themselves, lie in spasms,
their cheek and chest muscles like rock. I pass over them,
smoke them, whip them, revive them, send them out again.

Wise wind singer with a forked tail like white lightning
and your black pin eye. Paradise tern on her tail-long hair.

I am thankful. I accept. I take your offerings of pork lard
and the myriad flowers of the scissored palm leaf. I take.
I accept. But above all I thank you for the breasts in heaven
of my daughters of the island which is Nukahiva of the Marquesas

that you know as Herman Melville's green garden, his Pacific.

Some say he beautified this green back yard.
I speak from ignorance. I remember little.

18

PRAYER FOR ROSES NEWLY PLANTED

If you should suggest to a Native that he should make his garden
mainly by magic and scamp his work, he would simply smile on your
simplicity.

B. Malinowski: *Magic, Science & Religion*

Some have said they thrive in peat, some can't stick peat;
some have said spread the roots round, some all one way –
above all, again, let them not dry in the wind, lop off
the weak and wounded, eliminate all leaves. Obeyed them
all on the good day for planting that never comes I did,
bedded them firmly in this blessed earth on a warm day
(with rain). When craft has drained from the brain
and seeps along the fingers blind as roots – these hands
I guess are holy and holy the earth I wrinkle them in.

They arrived in fog from the floral mile a day away;
I can't even say I raised them on my ground – hardly
have any ground that I can own in this city, don't know
exactly the names of the gods of this borough,
the spirit of this street. Is it the blackbird, whiskered
with withered fly, that looks me sideways or
a pipsqueak from the rhododendron patches: robin or tit,
perhaps the worm, belted with generations round his waist,
the emerald greenfly ... the furry cockchafer?

Lords all, Ladies if it comes to that, to you commend
I do these unborn flowers: from my hands receive them.
I shall water, hoe, feed, mulch and fertilize – all
in their seasons, so I have fat blooms to blend, to blaze
the rooms of summer with and bind the breath of friends.
To this garden's four quarters I make amends: wounds,
cuts and grazes to my fingers take, let nothing harm –
mine be the thorns of your lives. Tonight, come rain,
come wind, I lie awake in my roses' arms and their smiles,

19

with the heart travel down to the scion, with fingers
feel out each root, every extremity, with the nails
grope at the clay and find my estuaries there.
In the city's ore: the blood of brick and stone's sweat
my brides lie down with me, in their deaths I achieve them.
I shall flood up and come to own this place altogether
and be the Nile of Hampstead, Alexandria Gardens, 33,
when what summer we have brings me to work again – Hello!
the first shoots titter and fingers crave the velvets of the heat.

BLACKFLY MELTING

Coating an elder tree's sparse ribs
a blackfly nursery
prepares for anschluss with the cream of buds.

The candle I use burns milder than I'd hoped:
the pests move their legs with such sloth
before melting to caviar.

My eye is too high, unhelped by loupe.
I have a god's vantage to view this inquisition
but a human heart.

Delphiniums in choirs
assure me I have done right.
This blue of kingfisher, mariposa, angel eye,

the daisy's gold nipple,
a clean rose billow, many pregnant shoots
assure me I have done right.

Hacked from the elder's chest, the charcoal ribs
break on the cuttings, meat-fly buzzed,
crumble, like bones in less perfumed pits.

SOME PEACE FROM AN AUTUMN GARDEN

Those rhododendrons careless builders singed
by your humble surgeon cut back now like amputated bravos stand
a shade astonished, and the brown covey, the bird ballet, is boughless,
has lost its dank parade. On this my tidy parcel, my square stage,
the ousel thumps and scrabbles in the sapless leaves, a robin secateur
snips longlegs, pigeons tip to their elderberry stingo like brigadiers,
brushing true sergeant wren down from his battlements:
what a bird mob is here! Is this peace?

The way the light layers through leaves like a knife through pages
draws my rose-blown Chinas here and I gag on them to crying sometimes.
This hugeness earth! We should burn down these rotting palisades,
establish communes. But Lord! my privacy! your privacy!

In the beds the rose Peace has the devil's own yellow cheek,
blows up like throat or rump of a Rossetti blonde when in full heat.
I can't really stand these Peaces can you? I must have others:
crimson gargles, or demoiselles' pink sniffs, to blend with them
and to make bowls of in old glazes Fantin would faint at and I
pour my whole life into. Would you dream a man would long his way
a lifetime through to a bowl of roses fixed just so?
Yet for me, when the light splits home, first sight of it is day.

Our dun bird-life subscription (God for the tropic blazes!) how sees it
parcels? And those steel phoenixes overhead, those sterling whirlwinds,
loud as knights in their liveries with the long world their lists:
how does their load see us – a glint, at best the flash of a hoe?

I burn the soldiers' limbs and a rich white smoke rises, fire-rimmed,
to signal that I am trapped in here and do not know how to get out.
If I were not such a cage, full of earth's armies, I'd shrink and go.

I need the rose Peace to seem meaner and what she stands for also.

FOR THE DEATH OF ANTON WEBERN PARTICULARLY

Sunday gardening, hoeing, trying to think of nothing but
hoeing – so that this at least can be an exercise in the true sense –
nevertheless I can think of little but the death of Anton Webern.
I just happened to read it. It just happened to be Webern.
One has ferreted out and written up at length how the Weberns
went out to dine some night with their daughter and their
(unbeknown to them) blackmarketeer of a son-in-law, shortly
after the American occupation. The G.I. agent provocateur went out
to block any escape. Just at that moment, in the black back yard,
the fragile Webern, out to puff a gift cigar, collided
with the decoy who shot him by mistake. Back home, not knowing
whom he'd killed, but withered by it, this kind man died of drink.

Sunday gardening, hoeing, I turn over the worms in their beds
and am shadowed by the blackbirds. And I have to ask again from what
body-stitching those worms are sundered and picked out writhing to die,
and from what soul-harrowing that Rome of blackbirds flutters down
to drill and gut the worms with javelin beaks, and in the fold of what
wedding of body and desire in Jerusalem I am conceived and born
to offer this show. I need to ask on what Sunday God first churned
his cauldron world in such a manner that we all deal death,
not knowing that we deal it, scarcely caring, yet dying of it too
from afar – in what stew God first mixed meat of worm,
feather and beak of bird and hand of man and what bubbles
send up each in turn to do the other in. And how, at last, the notes
composed by fragile Webern survive the boil and music in the bubbles.

THE EDEN FOXES

'And will you believe it? Seven foxes, seven!
on the lawn!' Said I: 'There will be lions (laughing)
and tigers and perhaps elephants next!' But thrilled
and thought to myself of the wild would be there first –
before the destroyers came in our guise or another.
And indeed, yes, a perturbed slant to the tulips and lilac,
must-drift, a stench in whiffs as of weed rot far off
and cold dinners: a gashed fish here, here a black bone:
'To the butchers and fishmongers they go; they are
everywhere now the rabbits are thinning of myxomatosis.'
Across the lawn, by the garden hut Eve played in
as a child, the savaged leavings of a hen, and as she passed
holding her child, a growl and coughs beneath it.
And I pass too but get not even a growl. Yet heaven's
Wind, as once He transposed Eden, kindles, though I cannot
find: the lawn is rusted with foxes, rufous with brush
and snap-jowl. To my mind the day streams with foxes like
fire. Who have drawn Eden there, salvaged, reaped again
down to the autumn grasses Eden in splendour – O that day
of scythes as He the Lord got tired of His rest and loosed
the Eden foxes! 'They, not the snake!' ... 'There! there!'

THE OMEN

We are in mourning for a nest of blackbirds.
They were born with a son to the house; we felt
fruitful – I would say: 'We have many children.'
I had discovered them while pruning an ivy; they were quiet
for half an hour before I came lip to beak with them.
I whistled scant tunes and they seemed to like me.
This morning I climbed to look at them. The nest was clean
and empty, the garden deserted by birds, I'd say hollow.

I would like to have been a manifold Tibetan phantom
to put a thousand gods' worth of terror into that cat.

Bird penury aches at the morning's navel
and all along the busy day. Could they be blaming me?
For we know the sea laps at rock all round the world
and drowns, or red tide poisons, whole colonies a day,
while beasts agonize on doped food: I saw a baby rabbit once,
barely got used to day, blind in a plague of froth.
But to have it happen here – as by the ivy's reach we knew
it would sometime – lays an ill omen on this normal house.

The world is eaten slowly by her peaceable cats
whose guiltless teeth stain with the guiltless bird rust.

THE CURE

Among the rugosas and the wild, hip-loaded, feather-leaved,
thorn-warning ones it happened, not in the law-abiding beds.
Hip-orange and white the damned thing streaked, with a grey wash
in its mouth, and I knew, spat Oh God no and ran to the patch.
The whole bird racket in there had maelstromed and swirled out –
all that came back, jilted, as if drawn with stump paddles,
was a float that had not yet stained air with the softest of greys.
Had never begun. Seemed to be swimming, discovering, looking about.
With an idiot's sloth. The beak opening, closing, without a sound.
Saving was out because of that red bared spine and the thickening syrup
at the beak. Now I shall not kill a fly the size of a pinhead, no.
My hand could not find its way through the thorns and cat claws.
My feet came down on the early wings; they swam still, swam still.
A big fly lashed on to the gash and held tight. I stamped
again to dye the ground. The whole bird universe with its one
soul shuddered and winced, I know that, and wings withered in me.
What horror-struck, astonished wrath like mine, when I am gashed,
will hammer down its terrible extremities to comfort me?

NOT ASKING THE WAY IN A PARK

Who has seen the trees in this park, I mean seen
and stretched his thoughts to their branch tips
where they bow over traffic like grandees – who,
cars dodged, path soled and heeled, has fallen a long,
long time to slower, altogether more harmonious, pace
and hovered, come to rest, on this manned bench, not that,
asked 'why, why the old pipe-puffer say, not the hag?' –

has said, for instance, 'on my right: a presentable, relatively,
ferret in spring's trash-can for what good grief?' or 'broadsides:
one ringed finger on a skirt pleat, well-wed, a honeycomb
to a hive of buzzing, drumming, hack and saw blond brood –
who would though, in this mist, let go if she could'
or 'now a queer with a westering dart at a boy who should
and never will' or 'then a clerk with autumnal teeth?' –

has had his life on his tongue and missed the salt
or any taste at that, hissed in his teeth 'shall I ever know?' –
hissed in this park, in this very park, 'I'll slow down so
at last I'll talk with them' – gone home, barmy with numbers,
crazed by the uncaressable, relentless scatter of fellows,
cursed them all for the pale niggers, sallow yidden they are,
pigeon-tossed so under a crass (but yet forgiving?) sky?

PERSEPHONE'S DOWN

She was so wondrously beautiful was she not?

On pale gold chintz: mahogany's skin,
pillowed on plush ('your hair's so greasy'
was their saw for years) and swathed in wool –
the furniture drowsy on its pins and needles –
I totter to the cliff of sleep and break no fall
with sheep-leaps.
Behind the windows' frosted shroud
the grizzled panes weep like widowers,
the sky snivels into its beard of trees.

There is scarcely any room left for beauty here:
my back is against the wall as she sweats light
before she drops through stick and stalk to her sleep.

Prise open the oyster of silence with crisp
creaks far out backstage cock blackbirds.
Flowers, such crystallized sweets, water the wind's mouth
and trees would beg hot soaks for their backs but for me –
all turns to surf and the sea at the source of the mind
licks up her calves and thighs towards my ends.
It seems I have never seen anything but her spine
grading away from me the russet waves of the leaves.

I said to her once: 'I am so happy, so happy.'

Two

OLD SAVAGE/YOUNG CITY

I

From the inner skin of my dreams,
from the womb's lining turned inside out,
where the soaring pine cone once nestled;
from the capsized backbone of my iron ship
that ploughed the rorqual, now a harpoon
thrust navel-deep into the fallow sky,
this knowledgeable heart, magic artificer,
convenes the mystery of all that I have ever known
and I find myself delighted again to belong to this world.

Streets like flexed muscles cannot knock me out:
I guess as far as power reaches, or indifference,
and then I have grown so used to sleep-walking
that sleep's no problem now.

Early I acquired the habit of looking for the eternal side of things,
tried to accomplish, in silence, what enthusiasts by the score
never even wished to begin. All for a smile's sake,
chivalrous above each proffered sacrifice.

Thus I cannot be frightened by these heroic tantrums,
this evangelism in the canyons of noon.
With trust in the continuity of all action
and stillness where the crowd core pulses;
frequently knowing I end a deed in its beginning,
tender in nurturing my small mistakes
in the daily quest for equilibrium between love and solitude,
I condemn them, knowing that I am ever of this life.
Delighted to belong to this world in my own autumn,

31

because I never take without giving in return,
never allowing a present even a flutter in my hand,
yet only reciprocating at the long long last
when the donor has forgotten what he gave –

for everything surrounding me forgets,
cities lose remembrance in their veins,
their ceremonial pattern fades,
their quick-step echoes die away,

only the shaman frolicks, mocking his own mask,
whole capitals crumbling while he counts his fingers ...

an honest servant accused of selfishness!

II

That which achieves its little ends by little means consoles me:
in a mausoleum details matter:

The way in which a nail mates with its wall,
a doormat yields under the feet of those who go in and out,
a door knob cools a sweating hand,

put me in touch with lives I have had difficulty in reconciling,
open the algebraic eyes of paradise.

III

There is not enough room in the sausage factories
so they take new measures and kill pigs in the street.
We do that, now and again, inside our community houses
but only when some important day of the gods is at hand.

Here there is no sign of the gods in the streets
and every one walks by without raising his hat.

Some pale eyes blink but forget soon enough.

IV

The solitary man responds to matter
by taking it with him,
anchored to his soles and heels.
Others wallow in their freehold muck,
deprived of the whitewashing dividend of visions.

He who laughs within himself as he gazes around him,
seeing nothing but his eyes' laughter in others' eyes,
bears his own problems on his own shoulders
like a diminutive circus of birds,
without ever travelling from one city to another,
ever crossing a street,
or leaving a room to go down into the street,
(and so forth)
whiling his dusks away going home,
recalling his own sky and humming a love song.

V

A body on the morning after love is a jungle of smells,
inexplorable as a swamp, its sex closed.
A city after two or three weeks of being lived in,
accumulating its more and more exasperated skyscrapers,
becomes a terrified hermaphrodite looking for itself.
Male endures, female forgets.

VI

Darker than my loves themselves darker than white:

Some Capitol unscaled by technicians has engendered them
and dropped them on the streets
where they change in a trice to black swans.
Then positive is negative again within the camera,
the roofs close in with the grace of trees, excluding light.

Chocolate-eyed Cassandras, marvellous with hunger,

the black girls glisten as they walk away
more naked than if they were naked.

VII

The professional suburbs are peaceful.
Mr Western goes home, forgets time and space,
puts on a docile dressing-gown,
recovers his absolute self,
wires roses to his love.

Unless she phones from far away to say that, tonight,
she flatters another man, the next night weds another
and so until this time next week or the week after.

This anthropologist translates romance to ritual.
Each footnote's rare, already obsolete.

VIII

Aeons of frustrated flight,
the queen's nuptial indifference,
profit us nothing.
By betting all on building, man alone destroys.

No eschatology distracts the ravaging bee
from voyage to the sun. But man eliminates
time's architecture in the plan,
each nail, each brick, each girder in the mould.

I remain, planted everywhere, like pine needles.
I slouch, unwieldy as a fossil beast.
I am the lodestar of all faces, the slumbering animal.

IX

A raven death hovers above the river
grey with sarcophagi.

If the other world, as some myths have it, were similar to ours
and if all the ocean liners went there together on a given day
sailing towards an identical fresh city
with legions of garish dead aboard
who would be helpless without their desks
and phones and sexy secretaries
or (talk of pleasures) without cigarettes
bitter and human by comparison with their smokers, still

somewhere before the latter end there should be pity for them:
the air might be yielding and tender a few feet above the water,
softer than in the whaling seas where coffins are of coral and amber.

X

My face, when all is said and done, looks like a city too,
each wrinkle a street more or less in shadows by the watch,
shallow or deep, depending on its traffic of emotions.

Sometimes I lift my arms to the sky like skyscrapers
to join in similar lament, with ships coming and going,
and sometimes my thoughts follow surprising thoroughfares
with very few crossroads and intersections.
Then my logic tightens and shines, especially at night,
for a wind-thrashed old lady walks by me.

She is as beautiful as love.

On the day the earth achieved enlightenment –
as it is said: each blade of grass shall know itself
knowing the wind it bends to its own purpose –
on the day our people went down to the sea
and welcomed in the dead from the breakers,
feasting them for a week with nothing withheld,
before they took them back again to the shore;
on the day the living and the dead walked hand in hand,
harvesting to themselves their far-flung fathers
who had heaved with the whale in the deep

and haunted with their wings the arctic hare,
on that day I was exiled and came to this city.

She is as beautiful as love.

Can I ever forget her? Tonight, sitting here, now, together,
we could be anywhere in the world, in any season, at any moment –
I have gathered her to my arms as the pines gather birds.
I call her mother and all her age-mates mother, as I once did,
I call her sister, daughter, lover, wife, and all, as I once adored her,
by the same token of oblivion.

I am profoundly lonely within myself, lonely in the land's bowels,
as lonely as a man can be ... but this is not her business.

Cities devour her face.

New York 1953 – Cambridge 1963

Three

ELY CATHEDRAL

O to laze and to lie down in my soul,
to rest on the hard light of a fen morning!
But pheasants scurrying, wet tails
tucked low behind them in the steaming grass,
tough crows choking the furrows' throats,
pigeons cooing into their breast mirrors —
beaks scratching their metallic image of the earth —
disturb the fields, ruffle the sky. The farms,
hugging their acres to their walls,
spit out thin populations, cycle or tractor mounted,
towards spine-breaking tasks:
their blood's still tea and mist
in the awakening tendrils of their veins.
Delicate animals, bred for a millionaire,
in Indian file potentially the paragons of motion,
touch empty roads with froth and whips
and rainbow silks. All at this early hour
remorseless glides into the morning's grooves
and rest is out. Why! over all the Isle of Ely
even the stones, virgin or cut, still wait
an evolution into higher states; even their queen —
the dream of immemorial saints, the sleep of kings —
at anchor: yearns towards the earth's high tides;
rich: she would sell her towers for Christ's limbs
and be as free as birds thrashing the sun
when, swerving, they turn winter over with their wings.

TO TELL ANDREA OF THE ÎLE DE FRANCE

Waking to a strawberry light
our dozen odd wealth of birds dins like lala!
– or can you say 'music' by now?

Darling the houses here are of grey stone,
except for a long barn pink as a birthday cake
and the trees are so free they can have many children –
you find the chestnut babies in rows between their parents –
the rows I'm thinking of lead to a cone-hatted castle
where an alchemist prince lives with a fortune in dogs:
they put him in a tower for *selling* his drugs, but he's out
again now. Oh and the prosperous farmers hereabouts
wear shining black velvet pants which bag round the popo.
You'd like a dress of that.

In front of the house there's a thick wooden beam
near the water mill stream that giggles in our sleep.
All the dozen birds breakfast on this beam. Nuthatch
gets through his breakfast a lot quicker than you
and greedier than you he whisks bits off for his granary.
Sparrows and chaffinches are well behaved and send no news.
Warblers are shy and stay in the reeds, the wagtail's tail's
too heavy – he can't make the beam. But I think
you'd like the goldfinch most: he whips the air
to a cream and falls over himself with excitement.

You see him best, the goldfinch, in the beds of cress.
Beyond the wood at the back of the house
where blackbirds arrow through daffodils and flan to cover,
in a small valley fisted by quarries of grey stone,
the jade and emerald cress lolls in its swimming pools
whose temperature never varies. The water gurgles up
from piped holes in the pool beds; it's good for cress –

the cress is good and itches on the tongue, you can't imagine.
Daddy climbs up on the hills, sits on the quarry's lip
and stares and stares at the cress until his eyes go green.

I'll bring you here one day and tell you of France.
I'll make the lilies on her blue sky frisk for you like birds.
You'll wear a black velvet dress and eat cress till you burst.

REMEMBERING BENARES

Famous is this Vārānasī which, having usurped
the extent of the abode of the three worlds, is
worshipped from afar ...
                    Inscription of Pantha, Benares

For one day only I stopped in Benares
and I've been there, on and off now, one year.
I soak in a river grey with ghost tears,
praising a sun as fierce as a torch of corpses
in the sky's muslin shroud.
As a body's proportions: ankle to crown
is the sky there; the feet are all that's earth.
What earth! If bodies from the sun's beginning
had sweated their brown juices in that earth
and the loam had been leavened like dough –
a cook god's hands squeezing sugar spires,
temple dome puffs and palace loaves,
towering cliffs like slices of a bridal cake,
lifting the whole dun earth's foundations
to set them round the skirting of the stars –
you would have Benares.
Aboriginal, scribed in water, dust and air,
are her women's gestures on the river banks:
you will find them in the Ajanta paintings
and Khajuraho sculptures, lust's circus.
That silk raining upon a brazen hip, that flash
of eye upturned, a dish for the sun's semen,
that breast lolling on flower necklaces
the day away tot's mouthwards, they are there
among both frescoed virgins and stone satyrs.
Parrots that once to some past Buddhahood,
their emerald wings upraised, bowed in salute
now nestle in a woman's navel pit
or hide her jet pudendum with their beaks:

more than one parrot were I in his moods
for lust and spirit both, so could I hold
thrice many loves in hand as I now hold Benares!
I remember of this city a bather rising slowly,
fresh resurrected in her clinging silks,
to thread the narrow streets with her tawny eyes
in a dust cloud seared to crimson and ochre;
at the wedding booth she begins her dance
while higher than her arms erect as spires
and minarets girating on her open palms
three doves, O whiteness manifest, purl wings
to raise a crown above her streaming hair.

A TWILIGHT FOR THE RAJ

Hail to the moving twilight of the British Raj at tea!
– though bankers breed bloater there than ever before
(population control's not for them). The tiger, whoever he be,
parted the leaves in India's hills through it all,
say from Clive to Mountbatten in one snarl, and parts them still
to rip the light that wombs each fat or scrawny wog
as he squats on the banks near the holy running mother,
beating his skin and linen dry of greasy sweats to swell her.

High above Victoria and her fistful of pets
buzzards outsoar the strutting carrion sun
and spy for offal still: 'I forgive you my friend,
I bless you my brother' he said, falling.

While at Mayo they smear each dawn with marmalade
and Kachenjunga's propped up with St Paul's game gothic
(not to run the puppies of Ootacamund into the ground)
sneak that to Siva pounding his mountains, score that and shiver!

(And let's be sure to bind in all the parchment voices –
those who chucked furloughs sitting for duck rosters in Sind
or numbered the heads of the hunters in the tribal hills
and pre-Anglo matrilineal clans in the trill and lockjaw tongues.)

'The crow was here my dear even before the wogs
were as Persilled as this in these turbans and coats,
who carry curry better than Minsky's wavering bums – though that's
all we let in at the club. The crow was here, his shambling hop
and thieving disposition at the picnic, when the rain
forced us under the screens the tiger parted, hush once, hereabouts,
as drops made a noise of languages in concert on the pattering leaves,
near sousing every spooky bug I feared in childing time ... '

When Babu's lover etched her breast on the sky,
with her hand to her hair to smooth the flowers there,
and from her belly the Ganges came as Siva withdrew –

'I forgive you my friend, I bless you my brother' he said, falling.

THE MOON IN NŌ

As when the moon hides behind clouds and sulks,
waiting for the world to warm, that she might,
by contrast, hold the sky in her cool hands,
so the principal actor – *shite* – refrains
and the flute goes on and on wailing and on
until the house steams and he says: 'Now,
I am going in.' He enters with imperial sloth
as the moon passes from clouds and snows
upon the hushing mountains, at the pace of frost
to glide down glaciers – those white feet
sliding so slowly forward, the toes uplifting,
then down again to slide and slide and slide.

And when, after a man's full age of silence,
next: preparation of belly yowls and mewling,
he has talked himself and the public
into his petrified white cold,
pouring his poetry upon our heads
like a fall of silver foil, a floe of ice,
he, hidden once again, from his frail bower
helped up by all, presented, now outshines –
that perfect face so lovely one could scream
as thick male hands deliver up the voice –
he seems the sun his ghost who clasped the moon
and trembled at her cold and so divorced,

sounds in the deaf, makes even silence sigh.

RENÉ GROUSSET WEEPING
AT THE DOORS OF THE SHŌSŌIN

'He had worked at the East all his life.'
He had drawn in through the sieve of his senses –
as one cannot draw in a lover even –
the mica dusts, the gilt, slivering woods,
the bat-dung crusted caves, the incense
lisping to heaven and her sister mists;
he had followed scholars to their lairs
and roared the midnight with them on their texts,
had trespassed on the dogged saints
and through them yearned to walk the burning air;
he had been almost by them at the last
when years face to the wall brought gapes,
hiccups and guffaws to their hallowed ease;
he had leapt with the mystics on their crags
like foxes as they made the peach or plum girls
and pomegranate brides – but on that land,
on the holy Asia, he had never set his foot.
For which reason, shortly before dying, he travelled
sunwards and came on his appointed day to the
Shōsōin. It is said, in that first museum of them all,
the keep of Emperors and their silken daughters,
that he knelt in the dust before the *Shōsōin*
and cried. Now some pretend beholders' eyes
failed also. I have it that that East, his only bride,
took him up in her arms, held him and cried with him.

ADAM PACIFIC

Zip down those pink-skinned Eden dummies cool
in the lush arbour of their lithograph!
Now take this photo, common black and white.
You find an old dark couple standing
5 ft 6 – not more. He: sandpaper-rough
through ringworm, strut-legged, with a long V
from waist to thighs, a horse's solid balls
and yam-fat penis tucked into their gorge,
a ribby chest, sunk neck and woolly hair.
The V again, inverted, falls from flat nose
to jowls. The eyes, upsaucered, squint
suspiciously over the nasal bone's trapeze.
She: sow-dugged and bellied,
a wisp of coconut beard at the crutch,
lowers her head towards a coiling snake.

Trapped in their photograph they stand,
fearful of spirit birds in my black box.
Do they depend upon the pink-skinned ones:
the fig-leaved humbugs, shamed in the rose garden
or well-bred snake, top-hatted for the nonce,
enouncing his stale sermon from the apple tree?
When clothes were taken to dark nudity
they wore them till old age granted prestige
and then they stripped themselves again of bark
and went about their villages in pride –
horse balls and all discovered to the wind.
When pale skins whispered evil in strange tongues
and claimed the use of balls was circumscribed,
they laughed and pointed at the snake's and said
all things that loved in loving made all thrive.

PORTRAIT OF A MODERN JEW

In the synagogue of my body,
in the flesh that is all Jew,
though that flesh has thoughts
which are all men's and not bound
by race or kinship, I am tall
and mostly bone, no fat slob I
to spit on and loose dirty names –
though had the fly been split
not so long since in Europe
and the covenanted skin revealed
(as once, in a foreign school,
when we'd dipped our pants in play,
I found out to my horror
mine lacked what all others had)
I'd be but bone and ash now.
Yet, with peace, where do I sing you
Israel? Taken, hand to cap,
all tarted up, some twenty years ago,
in a free country,
to the city temple – hoping
the light would grant
from ugly windows visions of my God
and sorrows heave us into heaven:
all I heard was chat
and babble of the market place.
I didn't know we had been trained
for that. I cursed at night
the Name of He Is That He Is
and waited for my veins to pop
and my tongue to choke me,
but stayed on ... By Law
we are not given form in paint
and decoration to depict the faith,

cannot imagine our long history
as others can – only our deaths
reveal us with a fiery star.
But I, alive and blind, in peace
where do I find and sing you Israel?

THE WEDDING

The company of those I had flown all my life
surrounded me again as if I had homed to them,
migrated back on well-worn routes. Do we know
which of his haunts a bird prefers? A secretary-
bird, haughty with parrots, a snake-crusher,
grey in the coloured riot, I await the bride.
Who came, lilting like a paradise, all of white
haloed, preening a little, so proud in her
slow sailing up that aisle as in some eastern
garden she knew best. And was suddenly by me,
I terrified by her white arrival on my grey bough.
We sang not but were sung through the black
bobbing – crows: bowing and bobbing, hissing
their psalms over us, we: passive on our boughs.
Leant over and were pecked and bibbed by crossed
parental wings as if to imprint and perpetuate
our 'instinct' for the nest. And then a glass,
like a snake's eye, in a tray below. Trained,
I shivered it with the thud of a talon,
nearly destroyed the nest it seemed to me
in the silence, and cried out a loud sentence
meaning: I take you fowl of Jerusalem to wife.
And all that day, and that night, I sang them,
whose calls or territories I owned not, and to them,
before the break, was like a balm, a flowing
like the seas between their homes – in a trance
sang them in for the last time to my bough,
filled their mouths with morning praises of me simply.

ISRAEL IN THE PARK

Where he wrestled all night with the angel
and in the morning was called face to face with God
to be confirmed in that his progeny would be as numberless as
the grains of sand on the shore of any sea
this side your clotted milk and grit-clogged honey Canaan

as had been granted Abraham – but by what sea, can you imagine?

I of the progeny take my progeny which shall bear progeny
for a walk in the park with others of Israel.
If we are a light to Gentiles it could not be said of us now
for these come too, with four-footed infants briskly
or meandering, buoyed out along paths by bipeds' hands,

queueing to get past a muddy patch, that the pram wheels
keep dry and 'your blankets on you or what will mummy say?'
some meet and hail and pass the time of day, as if leaning
on the umbrella one never takes on Sundays. *Goyim* days
for Harris tweed, school scarves and sheepskin gloves!

Do we say more than they say? Do we present said progeny
more solemnly to tatty beasts they keep for totems on the lawns?
or nose the air and hum and price the clouds, while progeny
squeaks, crows and whistles at the unclean brutes ('a salad,
rabbit! a carrot, hamster!') and whisk them off still shouting

'more!' down to the manna and the micturition of the waterfall
where there's much hushing and shushing witnessing this:
the covenanted skin must sometimes piss ... or to the burning bamboo
bush, brimfull of voices, brisk with childhood ghosts, or again back
to the 'quack, quack, quack' at the edge of the reeds
and the flurry of beak and wing in the bulrushes ...

to make this Israel?

– where I wrestled in my time of God, where I shed my wings,
where I fell from angels to this park of Canaan and became man –

but by what sea, dear Abraham, by what sea, can you remember?

FOUNTAINS ABBEY UNDER SNOW

A long time now I've been wanting to know
what gives these paradisial ships their silences,
their hush though hounded in the barking seas,
and I think I know now and take Fountains for example.
The sky's one leg weds earth to snow.
Birds, lunging for the clouds, feather it wildly but
that tower splits the arrows of their flight
and clattering to rest they cling to its lancets, fear to rise.
The sky takes its time snowing down, can hardly make the earth,
just manages in passing to cream an angel's cheek:
it is the winged tethered to their masts must make these silences,
circling above the smoking deck of the Misericord –
the only moving things down here are long since dead
where the souls of the white fathers shiver still
to brush along such soaring arches matins bound.

It must have been a fabulous sight for the hedge-sprung
and lane-delivered horseman from the cottages, shot suddenly
into this sounding plain, this ceaseless concert of God.
In the days when this vessel scooped them all from the depths,
the horse himself must have marvelled, bagged in his oats,
the surf brushed off him in his shrinking haze, and neighed
to the falls of plain-song, the rivers of prayer.
Meanwhile his lord made mariner among his dead.

My father's father could not get home to his graves.
He stood on a hill in shrivelled Poland once, looking down-wind
into another country combed by his wife for graveyards.
Far down she waved a kerchief when she found his stones.
Half-wrapped in the sky as in a prayer shawl
like Moses on the rim of Canaan he made his death-bed there.
Our blood laps with the tongues of war at Europe's shores,
we flee her armies and hide behind new names

if we've survived the dogs and common charnel house.
At Fountains under snow the rock soars high today:
I have no hold on her, no anchor in ankle-deep snow,
and cannot knit together the tendons of the sky.
Shorn of her vaults she swells and blows her topping spout
like Jonah's monster locked in Antarctic seas
while the prophet delivered huddles with grouse and fallow deer.

THE DELIVERY

On her bed the sea breaks in with a Sinai sound
we are deaf to. She thinks herself a ship, tempest-split,
spreadeagled on the waves. Sailors
in gumboots and oilcloths work in silence
to save her wreck and bring her into port.
She gapes at all her sides and the sea sings in,
wallows within to wash her bulkheads clean,
to bring her prize to the surface, her dead tongues
to our ears. In there are singing's keel
and each sprung stave of her own seed's suspension,
but here, but on the bed, it is all tide, all tossing,
all wave and surf and scum – the black rubber
of harbours, the rudders' plash and suck
and gulls guzzling under skull caps of oil.

Love's mount gapes dark and is torn apart,
Jerusalem laughs through all her open doors;
he comes in a rush of dirt and slime, the prince,
slithering like a fish in the gullies of Hebron;
his hair is a black web on my altar table,
night traps her stars in snares above Gethsemane;
his eyes glare out, his head swivels,
he is preening new wings now as he waits by Jordan;
the cord is cut as he bellows his orders,
the sky's trunk, his spear, he grabs from Enoch;
blue with the world's cold, brown with its ordures,
he looks about him, counting Judah's fee;
the star of David dazzles as Israel bows down
in Babylon's dust to receive her crown.

She thinks she screams but is silent really,
as the sailors press on her for her last cargo;
she thinks she creaks along her final course

as rubber hands reach in her for the anchor now.
She thinks she screams but is silent really,
like a body handled by the washer of the dead –
white on her white sails, tangled in her cordage,
she feels no backbone beaching through the sea's shoulders
while in each gap of breath abysses yawn
as round and boundless as the whale's grey hump
gashed with the furrow of her delivery.
But she is resurrected to hear him cry, the king,
and press him to her eyes where the sea still swells,
while on her thighs the spume goes the colour of earth.

A RABBI'S DREAM

I remember no breach, no infringement,
no scrabble for escape, no retort.
Only my knees printing the dust and I, bent
double as if with flatulence. Boots
ringing me round like saplings.
As if a fox trap had nipped
the tail of my heart I cried,
cried Kovno, cried Bialystok,
my private Lithuanias –
pale eyes with charcoal hair –
cried the genealogies of Eden
back to Jerusalem. But could not
remember verbs, knew no tough Hebrew.
As if my arse had suddenly snapped shut.
Black drapes on spindly branches
upheld me, encouraged me.
Sing by Babylon they urged, seize that harp.
I rose an octave, howled
the raven litany remembered now,
in the sound, the ululation
now, in the throbbing glottis

and thick tongue remembered.
And basked on the long beards
above the saplings
as I was howling, hard whiskers
on my cheek and tears
baptizing me: Son of God they whispered,
Saviour of Israel. And down the night I flow,
all my heart's drains cracked open,
down the night I palm these glyphs,
sleep not for nailing them.

SIMEON BAR YOHAI
TO THE COLUMNS OF LIGHT, A.D. 135

When they came out of the cavern everything that the gaze of
his son wounded the gaze of Simeon made whole. 'My son' said
Simeon 'you and I will suffice unto the world.'

From the *Zohar*

I am proud, yes. Let Abraham save half our time, I'll save
the other. And yet, you must be patient with flowers.
Suddenly they light up, suddenly catch fire.
When a wise word flares it rises to the Heart of the Day
where He shapes it as a calyx for yet another sky.
My general comes in his turn, reordering the mountains
round our teachers' graves, tiles to his tents,
bringing jars of starlight for the anointed's temple.
In the still places, when you least expect it,
such as birds' nests in the shadows, the beaks of hunger
gape. Not in the withering sun, too self-preoccupied,
but in Northern mists, in hanging cloud gardens,
tomorrow's Babel rises. Under a cedar's shade
the snake entwines once more old Adam's marching staff
and splits his tongue to a fork. And Adam at the gate
catches the angel's nape in that fork he'll not again let go
till Israel his name the winged night surrenders.

58

Who now has let in this man, rag to the floor below,
among these shields of the hosts, these hammers of the law?
Raw winds scour the armies and gobble up the trees
which are lashing the dusk with psalms –
gather their harvest of souls to print them on the sky.
My garden is vacant: the just have nearly all gone home.
On the thrones round the sky's house of study
the wise blind themselves with God, come down no more,
while Zion's rooster crows for me, the Jordan-winged.
My dwelling is a scholar's and suits me, a tower made clouds,
yet I have turned again to bridle the ass in the dust –
that is to say: I understood what had happened to me,
that I had tasted of the other world and I was afraid
and in that one moment saw my general relaxing in the sky.
Till the ass-straddling son pasture his beast in Eden
this garden still swells most and roundly delivers.
He straps my harness on the world to come.

ABULAFIA AT THE GATES OF ROME, A.D. 1280

I shall privilege you to be burned for the Holiness of my Name so that
you will be radiant in the world to come.

> From the *Maggid Mesharim*

ROME. I stare at these alphabets but they will not yield.
I pacify these gates where the dust is sifted,
shored up here like the lost tribes beyond Sambation
I looked for in my youth. They do not yield.

Come. I make of Rome my house ringed with rain's curtains;
I bring in the grasses from the threshold of the earth,
seek compassion on their behalf and they begin to grow.
Thatch this house with grass that my grass soul may have joy.

From Saragossa to Safed the world groans with my friends
who drain themselves daily with the wine of the Holy Name,

yet for years I have not met with them nor wept on their arms.
Let each one wake with me now under these stubborn gates.

We wear white robes that the white wind might play
with our spirits' sails and fan his storms on Rome.
We trace our breath like a kite string
till the tree of life reaches for our hovering lungs,

rake forage from the air as beasts dance in our loins,
shake from our limbs the binding alphabets,
shuffle them on the parchment here until our hearts grow hot
as the letters begin to mean more than any sage has told

and question what is Rome. The blind man's bread, this is Rome,
the deaf's libation who has not heard of her,
the pulse, the regular breathing
of those who have not even begun to dream that she might be.

The Lord's Great Name and His Wings keep company like persons;
we await their pleasure, envoys for tally sticks,
permute the letters with care, shift our limbs slowly
fearing to be crippled by wrong moves or a tic in the cheek.

In a clatter, ink and tablets fall; the whole city flares,
its limbs spark like torches, its flesh subsides to ash.
The Name lays out His gardens, makes floral inventories,
lectures on cultivation and fruitful husbandry.

The roots of Latin tangle with the Name's stock –
though roots stray far in sand some leaves sigh Hebrew still;
our extremities leap to cover this Roman trellis-work
even with parasite sucker or cankered rosary.

The city's custodian surrenders his keys
saying: 'Yes, I see, we blow with patience only:
if the Lord shoot not in everyone already, daily and minutely,
He must on no account, repeat, on no account come.'

The seals are broken, the knots are untied,
Rome resurrects before us, a woman open and willing,
and if I cannot wrap this city and her name in my Kabbalah of fire
how shall there be an end to time?

We are our own Messiahs in the details of our awaiting,
we stand before ourselves masked with His own face.
He holds the sword of Rome which has become a mirror:
in that dilating steel the image of my people is free to go.

THE MASTER OF THE NAME
IN HIS PRIVY, A.D. 1760

You should utter words as though heaven were opened within them
and as though you did not put the word into your mouth, but as
though you had entered into the word.
                                        From Martin Buber's *Ten Rungs*

By your permission, Holy Ones, I leave you at the door.
(The guardian angels stand outside waiting for him.)
Let them attend today: I feel our future.
Here I pass the woman water in me, the faithful liquid,
and with my feet in the mire my head reaches to heaven.
Suns rise and go down, they say, but let the misery on earth endure
and what need have these wretches to see my sin of sorrow?
As for the angels, they cannot care, obvious on their blazing rungs –
only we, in gowns of dust, move hidden up and down.

We dance our history out of an Eastern gate,
from the green corn soul to a blue window in the West:
take life from before your eyes, fool, as one lifts a hand
and you will see unearthly radiance rimming your grimy coat.
Down from the rusting North God's good provisions pour:
it is harder to provide, they say, than to split the sea
and twice as hard, they say, as giving birth.

61

So we are always passing through two doors: out of this world
and into the next, and out and in again.

Should you meet Messiah strike Him down, strike Him down
and be your own and your neighbour's. I hold the soul
of my dead teacher by the hand, who holds the hand of his
and so back to where Moses' lips move in the grave with ours.
He whose heart is the heart of Israel must not say
'This place does not suit me', for what are inches and feet?
but 'I am the place of the world and the world is not my place'.
If the way be a blade's edge, too thin for stick or prize,
if there be no hands, no feet in free space, how shall I retrieve?

The North has turned black: black for putrefied blood.
The convoys smoke towards it, the cattle trucks groan.
I see the bone and skin shops they'll open with our meat.
Here are the baths, the paradise fountains.
The doors will say with big placards 'Enter and be cleansed'
Children will play with their elders' fringes.
Stifling in the funny gas they will praise the Name I sell them.
This is the world to come, this and no other.
You are flushed into the Kingdom with gay gas sneezes.

NOAH ON ARARAT AGAIN

for Kit Smart: his spirit, his beasts in
'Jubilate Agno'

Gardens on Ararat? All's green on Ararat
fading to gold as sleep lays down the year,
powdering to ash as fire melts this sleep,
as here we garden, sweeping up the leaves.

Can we blame the rose for being the most beautiful thing in the world
or the Jew if he rot?
God how the autumn goes, how fast it goes,

62

in petal wine poured on the dry brown leaves.
This is a Jewish century you lot,
this compost is of falcon noses and shark lips.
I pried open young lips last night with a tongue
as sharp and darting as the hoe's in this new bed.
These are for the pot:

In my bones, in the marrow of my bones,
the humpback rusts the sea with one last thrash,
the tiger brings down whole forests in his fractured stripes,
the elephant collapses like a skyfull of clouds,
the buck stutters along the ground when hit, an aimless prayer.
Deserts burn out a snake some ninety million years:
his bones like ours are sheathed in Ararat.
My daughter's water, my son is fire,
we are all one man.

My daughter in green like the sea, in blue like the undersea,
lays down her hair in a crocus pool as the sun did on the flood;
in her head all the earth's brains spin like spring squirrels.
This is Israel's garden.
Fruit of my prying, your bucking and God's fastening,
this seed in your brown leaves my autumn love:
here must Israel harden.
The second, a boy, on Elijah's throne, can't hold his hoe,
yet is Israel's pardon.

In my bones, in the marrow of my bones,
the prophet in his sulphurous vein raves the old world along.
The people wake to themselves, rise from the dung,
from the sewage and guano and fish-bones and ashes
on a pyre as high as the flood ever rose.
The Lord builds His pulse into the creeping things of the deep,
climbs into trees with them and settles them on earth;
His stroke guides birds in the air, homes them to Ararat,
at right angles to the sun.

My son laughs like an imbecile in his happiness and in mine
my son is a baby of six months with two teeth on the rack;
in his head the prayers sing without their words
to Elijah's tune.
He'll lead beasts up the ramp to this ramshackle kiln
clutching at potsherds with his feet as an old man does
when he goes to prune
roses of fire with burning baby faces
in a late Aryan June.

Sweep old and new up the path to this Ark
whose base the curling whale belts like God's arms;
I lunge in you with her twin flukes
to leave you dripping, you last of animals,
with unborn generations in your thighs
or heave you up the sky on two bull horns
as ruined Moses rammed his Father in the sky
where He was making love with Israel in His brazen sheets.
The word is hushed at last, bones take no glaze –
the horns of Moses grew you know as any cuckold's would.

Love, they've at last shouted themselves to a standstill, asleep
with us as we turn;
they've cawed themselves to a whisper, a crackle of leaves,
with us as we burn:
my own hands at last are in the fire. As for my seed,
God will not mourn.

For we aren't very popular in this part of the world, my love,
and they won't say, when we light torches: 'You saved us, thanks.'
It remains for us to take in these late animals,
these few tillers and potters to scrabble in our ashes.
Ararat is on fire, my bride, Ararat is on fire:
the scholars won't even find the last ivory bones.
The Lord is jealous again and His soured wine
addles in your brown loins, my love, on Ararat.